Time

3:22

A.M.

BY SARA PISTOIA

Published by The Child's World®
1980 Lookout Drive • Mankato, MN 56003-1705
800-599-READ • www.childsworld.com

Acknowledgments
The Child's World®: Mary Berendes, Publishing Director
The Design Lab: Design
Editing: Jody Jensen Shaffer

Photographs ©: BrandXPictures: 4; Photodisc 24;
all other photographs David M. Budd Photography.

ISBN 9781623235352
LCCN 2013931434

Printed in the United States of America
Mankato, MN
July, 2013
PA02173

ABOUT THE AUTHOR

Sara Pistoia is a retired elementary teacher living in Southern California with her husband and a variety of pets. In authoring this series, she draws on the experience of many years of teaching first and second graders.

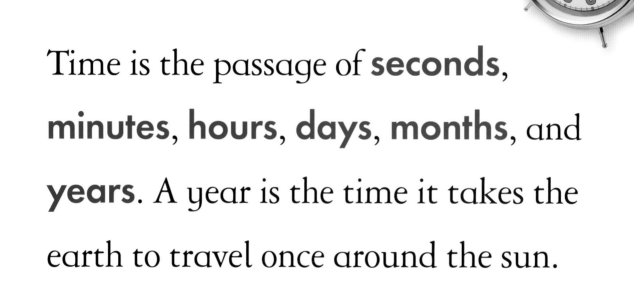

Time is the passage of **seconds**, **minutes**, **hours**, **days**, **months**, and **years**. A year is the time it takes the earth to travel once around the sun.

We use **calendars** to keep track of each year in months, **weeks**, and days. There are twelve months in the year: January, February, March, April, May, June, July, August, September, October, November, and December.

Did you already have your birthday this year? Look at a calendar and count the months until your next one.

As it gets closer, you can count the weeks and days!

Don't you wish you could have your birthday in every month of the year?

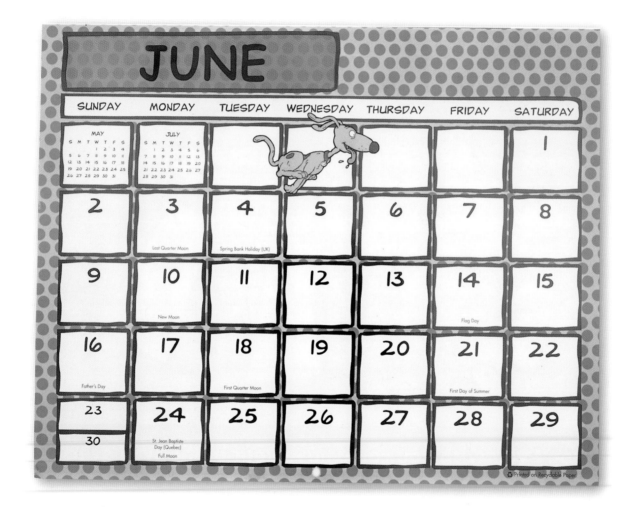

8

There are four full weeks in each month.

There are seven days in each week.

There are twenty-four hours in each day.

Can you name the days of the week? They are:
Sunday, Monday, Tuesday, Wednesday, Thursday, Friday,
and Saturday.

Your teacher can use a calendar to tell you when your next test will be. You'll count in days or weeks, not months.

Which daily and weekly activities do you keep track of?

To keep track of shorter periods of time, we use a **clock** or a **watch**. They tell us the hours and minutes of the day.

Do you use a clock to get to school on time?

If you start school at eight o'clock, the clock will look like this.

One part of the clock points to eight. Another part points to twelve.

Minutes and hours on a clock begin and end at twelve.

A clock has a **face** with twelve numbers. It also has three **hands**. The short hand counts hours. That's why we call it the **hour hand**. The hour hand takes twelve hours to travel all the way around the twelve numbers.

The **minute hand** is longer and counts minutes. It travels around the twelve numbers in one hour. The **second hand** is fastest of all. It goes around the numbers in only one minute.

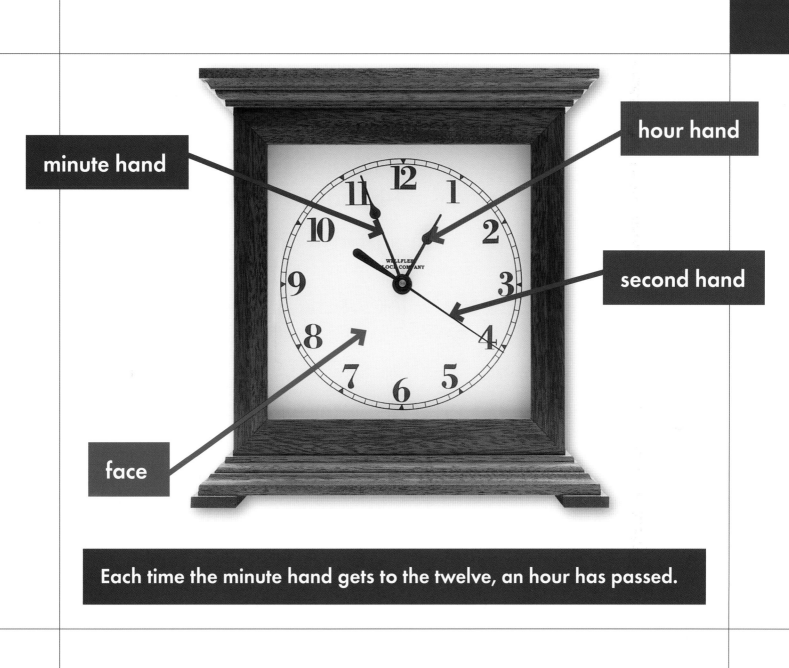

minute hand

hour hand

second hand

face

Each time the minute hand gets to the twelve, an hour has passed.

Some clocks don't use hands to show the time. They use numbers instead.

The numbers to the left of the dots show the hour of the day.

The numbers to the right show how many minutes have gone by in that hour.

We read this clock from left to right, the same way we read words in a book.

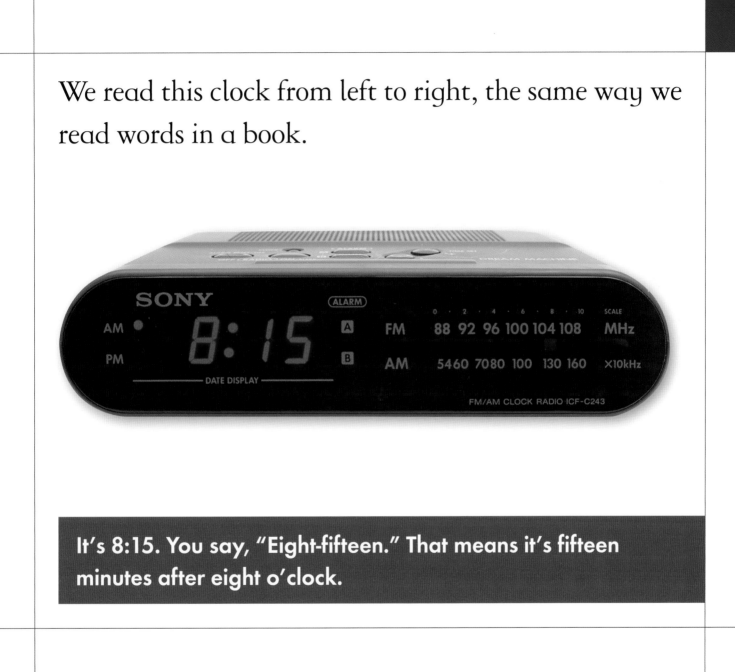

It's 8:15. You say, "Eight-fifteen." That means it's fifteen minutes after eight o'clock.

But what about smaller bits of time?

Runners want to know how fast they can go. They use a **stopwatch** to find out.

A stopwatch can keep track of very small bits of time—less than one second.

You start a stopwatch when a race begins. Then you stop it when a runner crosses the finish line. The stopwatch tells you exactly how long the runner takes to finish the race.

A **timer** keeps track of time, too. A kitchen timer is useful when you bake cookies.

How long do you think these cookies were in the oven?

People have always measured time in many different ways. We use time to keep track of daily activities. We use time so we won't be late.

We use time to think about the **past** and to plan for the **future**. What did you do last week? How old will you be next year? You can use time to think about these things!

These dinosaurs lived
a long time ago!

Key Words

calendars
clock
days
face
future
hands
hour hand
hours
minute hand
minutes
months
past
second hand
seconds
stopwatch
timer
watch

Index